CUENTOS WELA TOLD ME

That Scared the Beeswax Out of Me!

Priscilla Celina Suarez

About the Cover Image

"El Callejon Del Beso"
2011, Acrylic on Canvas

Artist: Chusy Ocala

DEDICATION

Dedicated to my abuelitas.

And to the new generation of abuelitas in my family – my mother and my tías. You have kept these stories alive, spooking even the youngest with cuentos we have shared for generations.

And to my nephews and nieces: Samantha, Eddie, Albert, Aaron, Diego, Anahi, Sofia, Rosalyn, Joey, Oceana, Cheeto, Fabiano Italiano, Ashton, Mikey, Laura, Evalyn, Alekai, Julian, Navia, Kailey and Tori.

It is because of you I am inspired to document these stories that have been passed on in our family, from one generation to the next.

CONTENTS

INTRODUCTION

Have you experienced an eerie chill crawl your skin and give you goosebumps for no apparent reason? Have you been haunted by a ghostly apparition you can't seem to explain? Has your abuelita told you stories about the legendary cucuys that have, for centuries, been a part of our Valley folklore?

These stories are simply cuentos many are skeptical to believe in. Leyendas my family has shared with me.

It is up to you to decide whether to believe in these cuentos or not. Regardless, they are intriguing and will continue to be told for generations on end.

Read on, enjoy, and beware of the cucuys!

DUENDES

Have you ever noticed how sometimes, while you are trying to sleep or at home by yourself, noises one would refer to as the house settling seem to suddenly creep into your awareness? You try to ignore the annoying titters and patters all around you. They are unexplained incidents one easily dismisses because they are of little concern. Maybe too insignificant to be noticed at first thought.

At times, it is the sound of a soft scratching on the floor or walls. Not soft enough to ignore, but when you to go check on it, the only noise you can make out is coming from the air conditioning unit or the ceiling fan.

Or maybe, it is the sound of light footsteps too soft to be real. And when you go to check the source of the noise, it is only your own subtle breathing you can distinguish.

Or maybe a slight knock on the window that sounds like branches hitting roughly against the panes. Except, when you take a look out of the window, there is no breeze visible in the night skies.

Have you sometimes felt a slight tugging at your feet while you sleep… but when you wake, you realize you are all alone? The only explanation is it must've been a sensation from your dream.

Or the feeling something is climbing your bed… yet when you turn on the light, there's nothing there?

I know I have.

Maybe it really is only our imagination playing tricks on us. Maybe there is nothing much to elaborate about. Mexican folklore, however, has an explanation for those baffling experiences…duendes.

Duendes are sometimes described as creepy little trolls or evil looking gnome-like creatures that make their abode inside the wooden walls, ceilings and floors of our home. These creatures are messy and have wild hair and stringy beards that reach all the way to the ground. They tend to reside in spaces where children live and are usually referred to as being traviesos.

Many things that mysteriously go missing in homes are blamed on these annoying little pests, as they are known to mostly take items that are of particular interest to children, especially toys.

If any unkempt children are around, duendes literally take it into their own hands to clip a child's toenails, usually cutting off skin in the attempt. Sometimes even removing the entire toe!

At nighttime, they spy on children as they play and find their faults to later try to convince annoyed mothers to give up their own young. It might seem like a long shot, but believe it or not, it has been rumored to work!

Saying all this might make it may seem I'm saying duendes despise children.

But, that's not true.

The reality of it all is they merely want children so they can have a decent meal.

LAS LECHUZAS

In southwest folklore near the borderlands separated by the Rio Grande River, lechuzas are rumored to be dreadful brujas who are so dedicated to their black magic, they sold their human souls to the chamuco in exchange for a set of magical powers that will last them a lifetime.

At night, they transform with the flutter of an eye into a monster with a bird's body and a beautiful woman's face, before flying and screeching through the night skies in search of their prey.

Yes, lechuzas are generally known to be barn owls found in many regions of the world. But the lechuza I am referring to is a stunning creature that comes out for a feast once the moon has set.

Her feast comes from giving sustos, which is when someone is frightened so badly the bad feeling remains with him for the remainder of the day. The greater the susto, the stronger a lechuza's strength will be before the morning comes.

People have been known to die from the shock of these terrible sustos.

When a lechuza finds her target, she will perch in a solitary location where she cannot easily be seen by the untrained human eye. From there in the distance, she will make either strange high-pitched whistles or the sound of an infant crying.

Anyone who is curious enough to attempt and determine where the sound is coming from is at risk of becoming an unsuspecting target. The lechuza will then swoop down and carry off the confused and horrified individual, who will be in for such a shock that he will be in a comatose state without a chance of running away for cover.

CHUPACABRAS

Many falsely believe the chupacabras, goat-suckers, are creatures that have come into existence in modern times. An alien species mysteriously transplanted from another planet and now hiding in plain sight.

In actuality, their existence has been documented for centuries, with original sightings being credited to the Maya civilization in pre-Columbian times.

My abuelita described the chupacabras as a species of vampires, strange creatures that prey solely on farm animals and never humans. Amongst their favorite meals are cattle, goats, pigs and an occasional dog.

Their existence became recognized in modern pop-culture after sightings were frequently claimed in the Americas during the mid-1990s. Claims from South Texas hit the media airwaves after a local farmer found his goat with mysterious wounds consistent to those of a chupacabra – clean puncture wounds on the neck region.

After that, claims were made by several other local farmers living in rural areas around the Valley. Few though caught a glimpse of the creature attacking their animals. Lucky them, huh?

Chupacabras are described to resemble large bat-like creatures that walk on their hind legs. Wingless, of course. Their long, oval faces sport beady, red eyes and razor-sharp fangs. Their weathered skin is a pale-grey coloring, almost greenish, with dark scales lining their spine. Chicken-like legs help them make a speedy and silent getaway.

Wait a minute! Doesn't this kind of sound like the description of an extra-terrestrial being?

DEVIL IN THE DANCEHALL

Susana was a catholic señorita from a small and rural town in Starr County. A beauty, the girl was at an age where her good looks came into form and she had discovered how easily she could get men to fuss over her.

Her favorite past time was spending time with her friends at a Tejano dancehall a few towns away. Although she did not drive and none of her friends owned a vehicle, nothing could stop her from going to the baile – even if it meant walking the lonely dirt roads wearing her favorite pair of red leather heels.

You see, dancing was a passion she carried in her veins. Susie's father and uncles taught her how to dance cumbias, huapangos and polkas at family gatherings, such as weddings, celebrations and birthday parties.

Her very first dance was at her tía Nidia's quinceañera. A natural, she was not yet six years old and enjoyed dancing with her cousins and family friends very much, kicking her heels with every beat of the tune.

Despite being from a religious family, she would go out of her way to attend dances, no matter the holiday. It was all the same to her.

Everyone who saw her dance agreed she was the best and a line was constantly in form at bailes, with boys and men waiting to charm her. Her father and uncles would look on, making sure her potential suitors respected her.

Girls prettier than her were jealous of Susie because of the popularity she had ritualized. Why, at one juncture, she even admitted loving dancing over anything else in the world. The fool went as far as saying she'd probably even sell her soul for the opportunity to go to a baile!

Maybe, just maybe, this was something she should have never said out loud. Especially not during the lent season, when it is the custom most Catholics willingly give up something they appreciate the most.

During lent season, only the drunks were known to show up at the dance hall. But one particular day in the spring, something felt different in the air. The evening humidity became thicker and the night sky got darker much faster than usual.

At the baile, the men present were the same partners she occasioned to dance with, except for an enigmatic vaquero hiding in the corner of the dance hall.

This stranger had such a strong appeal on Susie that she had no sooner seen him before she had thrown herself into his arms, eager to keep him from noticing any other girl in the room.

Tugging him out onto the dance floor, the house band played a polka as she let him lead her in a dance. He twirled her with little effort and laughed at her delight, seducing her with his dancing rhythms. At times, leaning into her ear to sing a verse from the song.

Complete strangers, they shared few words at first. But when confidence had stirred up in the girl, they found conversation came easily. He asked of her interests and she spoke mostly about dancing, the music she enjoyed and the moves she loved best.

Curious, the vaquero tipped his black hat with his thumb as he asked Susie what she would do for this passion of dancing. Being the silly girl she was, Susie told him she'd do almost anything.

He laughed as he grabbed her by the waist and slowly dipped her over, asking her if a dance with the devil would frighten her.

She giggled as she informed him just about anything was worth the leisure of dancing. He dipped her over again as he laughed with delight in a tone that made her unsteady. And when she saw his expression, she noticed something odd.

There wasn't much of a chance to think about it while he twirled her faster and faster around the dance floor. So fast in fact, she could hardly make out anyone else as they whizzed on by. It was sufficient to make her dizzy enough to ask her new dance partner to slow down.

While regaining her posture, she looked down at their feet and noticed the vaquero wore no boots. In fact, he wore no shoes at all. His feet were like the hooves of a horse.

As she tried to comprehend what she saw, his red, pointy tail wrapped around her thin waist. He laughed when he took notice of how stunned the silly girl was.

It took a good minute, but Susie now realized the oddity of his face.

It was red. Not a blushing red, but a dark maroon red. Devil maroon red to be exact.

Coming to a full realization of who she was really dancing with, she cried out for help, but everyone was too drunk to care. Untangling herself from his grasp, Susie's eyes widened as her mysterious vaquero planted a kiss on her lips, warning her he would be back someday to finish the dance.

Within a few seconds, he had puffed into a fog around her, leaving her behind with the vulgar scent of sulfur.

To this day, Susana has never attended another dance, nor engaged in one, not even at her own wedding. Anyone that heard of her story could hardly believe her.

I mean, knowing the girl, she was probably inebriated.

WHAT I KNOW ABOUT LAS MARIPOSAS

For over a decade, I've been researching the myth of Las Mariposas and their role in South Texas folklore. I first learned about their existence from my wela, Antonia De La Garza, who died a few years back in San Juan, TX.

Of all the people I have asked in the Valley, only one person other than wela has validated this myth.

This woman agitated about the end of las mariposas, their duties on earth and her own theory about why their stories have disappeared from our local folklore. Her name though, I am obliged to keep it a secret, and much of her information is too personal to disclose with anyone else.

Of all the sources I've studied at libraries and online databases, there is little to nothing mentioned about this particular breed of white witches. At random times, I wonder if this was a tale all made up by wela.

But then, I listen to other narratives of shamans and curanderos - men given the power to heal people. Their charms and ambitions are so similar to that of las mariposas. Maybe their associations had been of drastic consequences and are not remembered because of the discreetness these women took towards past provisions.

What I can tell you about these ladies is that they were once the sisters of lechuzas. But, that was long ago.

They inhabited the land in the shadow of their sisters, cautious and discreet regarding their resilient powers. Yet, people's natural instincts tend to anticipate who is enchanted with the supernatural forces. I believe it is human instinct for one to sense certain things, such as noticing the fear in the eye.

Same as their sisters were, the white ladies were born into handsome bodies, wearing their hair much below the waist.

They were born into the line of their female descendants. Mariposas were one-third human, one-third witch, one-third glorified. Living as normal women did, but capable of turning into butterflies resembling the breed of monarchs. That is, if the girl accepted to be baptized into her powers.

Already blessed with unnatural powers, once baptized, her charms bloomed to greater strengths with practice.

Until the girl accepted her path into this lifestyle and her powers had been granted, she was free from any particular duty. She had the choice to choose her endowments or to continue living a normal existence.

Las mariposas had a huge role to play in society. They were the angels that people unknowingly prayed to, the ones in charge of completing reasonable grants.

Because of the duties these ladies were bestowed, few of them actually married and had children.

Humans feared their qualities because we have trouble accepting what we don't understand.

It is for this reason they were associated with lechuzas. Not that their sisters were bad women. Don't laugh – I mean it! Lechuzas had simply been dispensed a bad reputation.

I wish I had more to tell you about these marvelous beings - but the truth is sources have run dim on this topic.

I mean, I truly doubt their entire bloodline has become extinct.

So I say to you, many females whose family has been in South Texas for generations have a chance of being a descendant, or related to one.

If that is so, all that you need to do is accept the duty as a mariposa and you will be honored with the charm. But, only if you are prepared for the responsibility that will be granted with it.

LAS LECHUZAS DE FALFURRIAS

Legend has it that las lechuzas from the Mexican borders relocated in the mid-1900s to a town named Falfurrias, TX. Although the breed of these black witches has diminished to a few, their reputation is still well known to most in our community.

Unlike their counterparts, las lechuzas have not died out and are premised to return to great power soon.

It isn't common sense why they were forced to make their home in this town, but it is rumored the collapse of the Reynosa Bridge in 1934 had an impact on the reasoning behind it.

Intuition tells me they have intentionally been keeping a low profile. Only, I can't even begin to figure out why.

These brujas are born as women but when their powers are unlocked, they have the capability of transforming into owls.

Though they are molded in folklore as witches that work only with black magic and bad intentions, this is not actually the case. They are half-human and half-witch, a characteristic most of us have.

Las lechuzas mostly have good intentions, but they could be trapped with the moods of greed, lust and hate. These are the cases in which their power turns sour and are typically the ones remembered by society.

Lechuzas shouldn't be cursed for preferring to work with black magic against the white magic of nature. They weren't born with the power of both. The white magic they know to use has survived in them from the teachings of las mariposas, their sister counterparts.

Do not blame them if their craft has harmful consequences on others. You don't know what it is like living with powers that are discriminated against but hypocritically called upon by commoners who don't let the charms of these brujas die out. Lechuzas, they have stronger emotional states than you or I can possibly cope with.

Don't bother the brujas with your foolish requests. They can abuse their powers to keep you from annoying them. And trust me, this is not done in a pleasant fashion.

If you ever plea for one, it can't be known which particular lechuza will answer your call. Do remember though that each bruja, just like a normal person, has a different personality and intention. After all, lechuzas are our sisters and mothers, aunts and neighbors.

What I am trying to say is, call only when it is truly a great need.

To call them out, you have to speak in a firm and demanding, but sincere voice. Use a rope made out of horse tail and tie seven knots that are less than an inch apart. While doing so, recite the following chant after making each knot:

'Woman of disguise,
lady of dark charm;
sister of white light,
listen to my call.
come fly in soft hue flight,
I do not fear you;
craft of blood in me,

listen to my call."

You will need to repeat the process, but backwards. Do so by saying the chant before untying each knot. Please do not make a mistake in this process of calling them out to you because you might accidentally hypnotize them and they will hurt you instead.

If you are successful in calling them out, do not be fearful - do not risk offending them.

I am sure that sometimes, at night, you could hear them scratching your roof. Do not shoo them away because they need to take breaks between long flights.

And they may just be carrying a good omen for you.

THE GIRL WHO BECAME A MERMAID

In our culture, Good Friday is a holiday taken seriously by Catholics. Amongst the accustomed beliefs for this day is that of not showering until the day has passed. The reason for this being that for faithful Catholics in Mexico, the water signifies the blood of Christ.

Accordingly, it would be malice to wash oneself with his sacrificial blood.

As a child, I couldn't even begin to comprehend the reasoning behind this. But, wela had a manner of sharing stories to convince me to obey old customs.

She told me of how long ago, in a town near the Gulf of Mexico, a young girl named Manuela experienced the curse of bad judgment.

Just like me, year after year, she had been warned not to shower on this certain holiday. She should not even wash her hands or face. She was aware of the significance it was to her family she follow tradition and she dared not to challenge them, out of respect.

At Sunday mass, Manuelita was informed of the bad things that would happen if she disobeyed these traditions.

Over and over, she heard the lectures of how disobeying would lead to her hair falling out until she was bald, teeth rotting until they too fell, eyes that would go blind, fingernails that would go black, skin that would shrivel and so on.

As she grew older, she would roll her eyes at these tall tales because when no one would see her, Manuelita walked behind the house to dip her face in cold water. It would have been embarrassing to have people look at her dirty face, so it didn't matter to her what the warnings were.

When this girl had married, things were different. Now she was the woman of the house and could do as she pleased without fearing the lectures from her parents.

Manuelita did not know what was waiting for her when she decided on this particular Good Friday, the first one as a wife, she would bathe in the river near her home. Regardless of the skepticism she felt, her vanity won her over.

As the morning rolled on, she walked over to the fresh waters and sunk her body into it. Just as she predicted, none of that nonsense she'd been told her entire life had occurred. For a long while, she swam in the water that quenched her skin in the most comforting way, for it was the freshest she had ever experienced it to be.

When the afternoon sun rolled in her husband found her in that same spot and frowned at her foolish deed. He told her to get out of the water and pray for her sins the rest of the day.

Her retort was she didn't have to do anything she didn't want to do. When seeing how angry he truly was, she reluctantly tried getting out of the water until Rodolfo's astonished expression made her realize what had occurred while she wasn't looking.

Without warning of any sort Manuelita had transformed into a mermaid, unable to leave the water that was now to become her permanent home.

Her legs and feet had fused together and had become a pale, scaly fin that splattered water all around her as she panicked to get out of the river.

Ni modo. Oh well.

She knew this was a punishment for doubting what she had always been warned about. She had become a sea person who would never again walk the earth, who would never be entirely human again.

When people heard of what happened to her, they shunned her disgraceful acts and denied her any pity. Instead, society marked her as a curse and refused to go near her when she appeared in the river. The shunning had become so evident that eventually even her parents and her husband had become so ashamed, they too refused to go near her when she called out to them from the river.

With time, they outcast her from the nearby waters because she belonged nowhere near the land as she was now a creature who had no business associating with humans.

Nobody knows what happened to her afterwards. It has been assumed some hungry sea animal made her into a tasty meal.

It is now said her punishment is waiting to repeat itself to a rebel disobeying tradition. This is how, for generations, children have come to understand the implications of not following customs practiced during Good Friday.

THE CURSED DAUGHTER

Somewhere in northern Tamaulipas near the South Texas border lived a spoiled daughter named Jasmin, the only child to her parents. From when she was a baby, she had been treated like a little princess and her parents had no heart to refuse whenever she asked for something.

When they went to town, her parents would purchase new patterns for her dresses and they would buy her the freshest sweets from the local bakery shop.

Sometimes, when they did not have enough to purchase Jasmin what she wanted, she would throw a tantrum and roll around the floor yelling and kicking anything that was in her way. Out of embarrassment, her parents would eventually ask the small shop owners to credit their account so she could have things her way.

As she grew, the girl had become a difficult child and a problem to her parents, disrespecting everyone she met. Her attitude had become so disgraceful that by the time Jasmin had become a young lady, her own parents had begun loathing her. Maybe it was their own fault for never teaching their daughter the world did not revolve around her.

They knew she was not to be trusted and believed the rumors being spread around town about her being more than a flirt.

One particular evening, while her parents were still furious at her for having arrived past midnight the previous night, she asked them for permission to go to a dance. As a punishment, they denied her their consent.

Not that it mattered much to a girl who had no respect for her parents.

So, of course, this terrible daughter didn't really care about what her parents said and decided to go to the dance against their will. She dolled up in the prettiest of her dresses and parted her long hair to the side, aware of how beautiful she was.

To avoid an argument with her parents, Jasmin jumped out of her room and headed straight for the door. Catching sight of her as she ran from the house, her mother yelled out to her, "Que te trague la tierra!" This phrase meant "May the earth swallow you!"

At that exact moment, the ground opened and swallowed the bad daughter alive. She disappeared without a sound.

Despite the numerous attempts to dig Jasmin from underground, she was never to be found. And her mother lived with the regret of cursing her only child. Even if she was a nuisance and a terrible person.

The morals of this tale are obvious.

Obey your parents so they will not curse you.

And never say something you do not mean, as it may just come true.

THE WOMAN COYOTE

It was a small pueblo outside of Nuevo Laredo that attracted Cuca. Not many people lived in the area, making it a good settlement for the solitary woman to build an isolated home. She particularly appreciated there would be few nuisances from the nearby townsfolk.

It is not exactly clear where she came from. Cuca never spoke much about herself, or her past.

All that is remembered is she came to town on a winter night, when it was particularly dark, with no bags or garments other than the ones she wore. She arrived on foot, which confused everyone since the nearest town was fifty miles away and nobody there had ever heard of her either.

That same night she arrived had been hit by thunderstorms lasting for more than a week and was followed by a disgusting plague of mosquitoes.

It wasn't long before this mysterious woman had built herself a small cabin.

What wasn't clear was how the place had been built, if she didn't have help or equipment to cut down the trees or to hammer the wood. Even more of a mystery was how all work had been completed in a single weekend.

Soon after having built her home, she befriended her neighbors by inviting them to weekly dinners that stood out as the best ever held. She would often cook a buffet of meats, steamed vegetables, a variety of breads, fruits and pastries – a pleasantry not common to the hardworking ranchers in the area.

But, Cuca owned no animals of any sort. She had not yet grown any crops from which to gather her vegetables or fruit. And because her only mode of transportation was walking on her two feet, it was obvious she hadn't gone to another town to buy the meals.

Nobody dared question her about these oddities.

There was something about her character everyone feared, but nobody could quite point out exactly what it was.

Rumors began spreading she was a witch of some sort. This was the only explanation her neighbors could come up with. After all, she always seemed to know what the weather was to be like and never became ill from the odd epidemics that routinely began to affect the community.

When it was discovered Cuca had a potion that drove off any illness, people hoarded her home for the cure and were amazed they had been told no lie. Before long, it was also discovered she could read the future by observing the lines on one's palm, and knew of secret potions to change a destiny.

Strange things happened to those who spoke badly of Cuca or refused to listen to her. They would become ill with bleeding blisters, stench like a rotten animal, or turn white haired. Unless they went to apologize to Cuca in person, there was no hope of getting better.

Because of the wrong doings she enjoyed, the rumored witch was avoided to the point where soon nobody bothered to visit her.

That is why when she left town, nobody noticed.

One day, she returned to the outskirts of town on a mule with a couple of children by her side. The boy and girl wore no shoes and were disheveled, probably from a tiresome journey. It was much of a coincidence that thunderstorms haunted the land for days after her presence.

When asked about her new company, Cuca explained the young Lucinda and Lazaro were her niece and nephew and would to be staying with her for a few weeks.

During those weeks and out of nowhere, a small group of coyotes began showing up to attack the cattle and chickens. There was a contradiction in this, as coyotes were not native in the area and no tracks were left behind to prove their being there. Soon, even the mules began disappearing.

Until these occurrences took place, the townsfolk hadn't considered guarding their herds at night, there had never been a need to. But a plan became necessary and families rearranged their daily routine so they could sleep during the day and guard their herds throughout the night. It was a practice many picked up and for many weeks there were no attacks on animals of any sort.

Not much later, they heard news of how a neighboring town had now been hit by the attacks on their herds. Little by little, after the attacks were no longer occurring in their area, people went back to their normal lifestyles and tried to forget about the incidents.

Not much had been heard about Cuca or her niece and nephew, and it was questioned whether she was still in town. But no one dared bother her, out of fear.

A year after Cuca had first appeared, a full moon was observed. That night, a local farmer heard his cattle making a ruckus. He quietly sneaked outside with a rifle, predicting the coyote had returned to eat his new herd. He had been quite correct because as he crept around, the farmer caught glimpse of a huge coyote feasting on a calf.

As he aimed to shoot the animal, it heard him and began to flee, and the farmer struck a hind leg. He made little commotion the remainder of the night but kept a good watch over the place, expecting the coyote to return. At the rise of the next morning, he went to sleep after a long night and did not wake until the afternoon.

It was such a coincidence Cuca decided to depart from town to find a decent place to live. She had made a great fuss before leaving as she explained a maniac had injured her before dawn.

According to Cuca, she had woken early to wash clothes when out of nowhere, a bullet struck her in the leg. She made an uproar about how some fool had ambushed her.

That afternoon, the farmer arrived in town and told people in town about how he shot the famous coyote that had been eating the cattle. He carefully detailed on how it devoured some chicken and a calf, and how he shot it in the hind leg before it got away.

Everyone was in awe after hearing the news, believing the possibility of Cuca having been the coyote.

Since then, not a single coyote has appeared to attack the animals.

But when stories of the feared woman are told, she is referred to as Cuca Coyote.

COYOTE EYES

As a child, I often enjoyed questioning wela about cucuys and leyendas she might've heard while growing up in Mexico. Coming from a culture rich with traditions and history, she had many stories to share with me and particularly enjoyed giving me the chills with her cuentos.

One of my favorite topics for her to story tell was about animals, especially about coyotes.

I've never seen a coyote up close. Actually, I've never seen one at all. But wela enlightened me with details about how their eyes are sly and yellowish, with a gleam resembling burning coals.

Wela once explained to me that many centuries ago coyotes had the eyes of a dog. She clarified it wasn't always so.

A long, long time ago before even wela's own great-grandmother's grandma had been born, a solitary coyote was passing by the house of an

25

old widowed woman minding his own business as he strolled the monte.

Back then, coyotes were friends of ours, just as a dog is.

The viejita was sitting in front of her fireplace, bulked over herself and sobbing loudly. She bent her head while she cried and cried, "Ay! Ay! Ay!"

When the coyote heard her cries, he became alarmed about her and decided to peek into the window to see if anything was wrong. Noticing how the old lady was bulging, moaning and in some type of pain, he believed her to be ill. Feeling sympathetic to her cries, he took a quick leap through the open window to help her out.

As he loudly thumped onto the floor, and not aware of his intentions, the viejita panicked and believed him to be a thief. She reacted in her own defense without any hesitation and pulled out the coyote's eyes with her bare hands, throwing his eyeballs into the burning fireplace.

She ran out of the house, yelling out to her neighbors about how there was a thief in her home.

Because the coyote could not see a thing, he poked the hot fire for his eyes. After a long and painful search, he finally pulled them out, with flames still burning them. He placed his eyeballs into their sockets but the anger he obtained from this experience has never let the flames die out.

For his good intentions, the coyote was wrongfully condemned.

To date, the coyote continues to hate us for the burning of his eyes.

NAHUALES

Nahuales are said to be humans with the ability to morph into a multitude of animal forms, such as a bat, donkey, cow, pig or snake. Throughout history, nahuales have been referred to as witches, wizards, and even aliens.

It is rumored that centuries ago, these beings had been transported from another world and have talents of the extraterrestrial.

They only eat raw meat, a motive for their shape shifting, and hide in plain sight.

Here is the story of Manuel, who tells the story of the day he encountered a Nahual living in his home:

"My name is Manuel Córdova Favela. I am an old chap from Matamoros.

I have no children with me because they all left to cross la frontera.

It was during late fall, about ten years ago, that my chickens began to disappear. My donkeys and pigs also began to disappear soon after, one at a time.

I said to myself, "It must be my greedy compadre, wanting to not use a single one of his animals for dinner."

My wife told me I had to go speak with Don José and demand for him to pay back what he had stolen. I had no doubt of his wrong doing and planned on confronting him myself.

I waited for the morning hours to come and went to pay him a visit, positive I'd find him at those hours. Indeed, I was correct, because when I got to his home Don José was still sleeping.

That was suspicious to me, as just the night before, another donkey had been stolen and this man is usually early to rise. I woke him up to let him know how upset I was. My compadre denied stealing anything from me, and even though I wanted to believe him, there was nobody else I could put the blame on.

He refused to replace a single missing animal and told me never to return to his home. I warned him to never return to mine either.

I was very angry after that and rushed back to my home in a hurry. This is how I caught the off-guard pig eating a donkey.

I was very confused by this. But out of curiosity, I walked closer only to notice the pig had no tail and was walking on its hind legs.

The pig was also singing a song of 'No Tengo Dinero' by Juan Gabriel.

Realizing the pig was singing, I instantly became afraid of it and walked backwards into the house, ready to get my weapon.

I called out to my wife and from outside heard her ask me what I needed her for. I peeked out through the window and asked her to come inside the house.

She responded, telling me to wait a minute, when I noticed the pig was speaking with her voice. I began to fear the pig had eaten her, until it transformed into my wife.

I was frozen with surprise and when she came into our house, I ran out to my compadre's home to let him know what had occurred. He convinced me it must be nerves and after a few days, I decided to go back home.

When I returned, my wife had abandoned me, and I have not seen her since.

Maybe I have, but not in her human form. And to think, I lived with her for thirty-two years without imagining what she really was!"

THE VANISHING GHOST

Carlos and Sulema Palomos decided to leave their Reynosa home for a life in South Texas. It was their intention to give their four sons opportunities American communities were popular for providing. It had taken them months to find a residence to rent because they had little money to buy or build one.

The house they would live in was made out of an old wooden frame, with little appeal to the eyes, but big enough for the family. It was located directly in front of the old town cemetery, right off HWY 83. Back in the sixties, the grayish house was the only site for miles off that road.

The journey to their home was only a few hours away and all the Palomos clan was excited to begin their new life. Most of the trip was spent with them singing old rancheros and giggling in anticipation of their future.

Sulema was so proud of her boys and relieved they so willingly accepted this change. She knew they'd miss their family environment back in Mexico, but also knew they understood the change was for their well-being.

They had not anticipated the change in weather on that day of their move. The closer they were to their destination, the colder and wetter the atmosphere became.

Within minutes of arriving in Texas, everything took a drastic turn. The clouds became black and thunderous. The road too dark and risky for Carlos to see as he drove. He couldn't pull to the side of the road and stop the journey because the boys needed shelter from the hail and lightning.

The truck was too small for all of them to fit inside, so the boys sat in the back bed. They huddled together so the thunder hit their backs and not their faces. Sulema cried from worry inside the truck, anticipating the worst, like a mother does.

All in an instant another car smashed into the truck, spinning the vehicle into a tree and causing a huge ruckus. Just like that, the four boys flew off the truck bed, dying on impact.

Their parents escaped the incident without a scratch, but scarred with the agony of their loss.

Several years had passed when Sulema discovered she was pregnant for the fifth time and cursed the fact this child would be born to her. She preferred never to have children, nor suffer the pain of motherhood again, as her spirit had been killed with the death of her sons.

Besides, she was waiting for the day to die, to join her children in the afterworld. With resentment, the baby's term was carried out.

Carlos, on the other hand, was overjoyed to hear of the news. To him, this baby was a gift from God to replace what had been taken from them.

He knew his wife hated the baby in her womb because it postponed her leave from this world. Night after night, this father prayed his wife wouldn't do anything drastic and that she would learn to love their new child.

His prayer was heard because on the day Sara was born, Sulema's hatred towards life and the child vanished. The moment Sulema laid eyes on the baby girl, her heart grew to a size it had been in what seemed like a previous lifetime, and filled her with the love and compassion she had forgotten existed inside of her. The only fear that haunted her was losing another child.

So night after night, she prayed Sara would never be taken from her side and that her sons would forgive her for staying behind in this world. Carlos and Sulema gave all their hopes to this daughter of theirs, as she was the last child born to them.

At the age of seventeen, Sara had lived close to a decade longer than her eldest brother had. She was raised with a strong faith and respect towards God, with a strong character of love and innocence. She was beautiful in many aspects, especially in her appearance. Like her mother, she had long black hair, tanned brown skin, large green eyes and a naïve but seductive stare.

These attributes easily handed her the title of popularity and seduced Jordan from the first instance he saw her. He was a bachelor twice her age and with a multitude of females throwing themselves at him. Being so handsome and wealthy, Sara was intrigued.

Jordan's flirtation was just for fun, as it was with any other girl. He seduced her for a fling, aware of her innocence, and she easily responded to his promises of much more. Blinded by this feeling she lied to her parents that Emily, a friend of hers, had invited her to a birthday dinner.

Sara looked beautiful in her pink sunflower dress her mother had sown for the occasion, blushing with excitement. It had already been planned she'd meet him on the edge of the road, a few feet from the house, and would wave him down when she saw the car lights. She conveniently hid in the sugar cane field until he came by.

Sara jumped onto the street when the car lights shone, blinding her, and she assumed it was Jordan. What a tragedy it was when the driver of the car turned out to be old man Santos on the way to visit Carlos.

Because the road was so dark and he was driving rather fast, the old man hit the girl with the car. She flew onto the gravel and passed away instantly.

Years after Sara's death, Sulema was in her bedroom crying for her daughter. A young man knocked on the door and she reluctantly went to answer it. As she opened the door, she asked the young man what he wanted.

He told her his name was Miguel and that the previous night he had taken Sara out dancing, but forgot to retrieve his jacket. Sulema slowly looked him in the eyes and angrily told him, "You should be ashamed of yourself for playing a cruel joke like this on an old woman!"

Shocked at her reproach, he assured her it was no joke and simply needed his jacket back. She responded it was impossible because her daughter had been dead for years, and he'd probably mistaken the house.

Miguel assured her it was no mistake. He was certain this was the same house Sara had asked to be dropped off at.

The childless mother asked him to describe the girl, certain it couldn't be her daughter he spoke of. But when he described her very image, wearing a pink sunflower dress and having a cold body, Sulema grew curious. She asked him where he picked her up and he replied it had been on the road, by the sugar cane field.

She remembered her prayers, begging God not to take her daughter from this world.

She asked Miguel to follow her to prove her daughter was buried and his joke wouldn't fool her.

But as she led him to the graveyard, footprints marked the path. And, on the cross marking Sara's tomb lay Miguel's blue jean jacket.

It is said Sara's ghost travels that same road every night. She appears only to men traveling alone, asking to be taken to her first dance.

Don't be afraid if you find her jumping out of the sugar cane fields. The girl won't harm you. She just wants to be taken to a dance.

She haunts this world only to please her mother's prayers of not losing another child.

LA LLORONA

La Llorona has haunted me since I was a child.

Whether it was her shadow appearing by a banks of a lonely canal, a cold breeze coming from the ocean's waves, or a solitary swish in the wind that spooked my ears. Her ghost is a mixture of mysteries to me. I've never seen, felt or heard her, but I always imagine her to be there.

The myth of The Weeping Woman is a widespread legend in our South Texas folklore, passed on to me by wela, who had heard about her from her own abuelita in Mexico.

It is always the tale of a woman hunting and searching for the innocent that stray alone by any bed of water at late hours.

Although several variations of the tale exist, the basic story tells of a beautiful young woman by the name of Maria, born to a humble family near the Rio Grande River. Charmed by a wealthy man twice her age, she ran away with him, against her parent's wishes.

He took her to live on a remote ranch near the river, where she spent weeks on end without seeing him, or any other person. She gave him three children – two adorable daughters and a dear son.

With time, his visits seemed to come less often and the money he gave to support the family had to be stretched out a bit more. It became a struggle to keep her children well fed and dressed.

Later, the visits just seemed to stop altogether.

Maria was alone in a secluded spot by the river and was in need of financial help from the father of her children. She decided it was due time to seek him out at the town he worked in to check up on him. Maybe he had fallen ill and had no way of getting out to the ranch.

It didn't take long for Maria to figure out the father of her children was a cheat and had lied to her from the very beginning of their relationship.

He was already married to another and had children her age. She was his secret and he never meant to acknowledge his relationship with her. That's why he kept her secluded, far away from prying eyes.

In anger, she raced back to her home, entranced in a furious rage. When her children cried out they were hungry she threw a tantrum, pulling each child out to and tossing them into the river. One by one, she led them to their misfortune, waiting for their shrieks to die out before tossing in the next child.

It took a few days, but eventually, Maria's temper subsided and she awoke from her trance. Instantly aware of what malice she had done to her children. Mad with sorrow, she foolishly believed there was a possibility they might still be alive and searched the river banks every single night. Never giving up.

Until, because of her sorrow, she drowned herself in the river too.

Maria is not permitted to enter the afterlife until she has found her children, forced to wander the earth for all eternity, searching in vain for her drowned offspring. Her constant weeping giving her the name of La Llorona, The Weeping Woman.

It is said her form could be found throughout the region, seeking her children. Sometimes grabbing children who go wandering alone during the late hours and keeping them as her own.

Legend has it that when a child crosses her path, La Llorona will run to grab him while crying out "Ay…mis hijos…mis hijos!"

LA MANO NEGRA

La Mano Negra is a legendary creature that has roamed the American Southwest and Mexico for at least a couple of centuries. This hand creature is rumored to be evil and is said to have been cut off a man who was burnt at the stake by his family and friends after he was accused of practicing sorcery.

At that time, it wasn't uncommon for those accused of witchcraft or sorcery to be burnt for their practices. The ruthless thing is that once accused of such things, a person was not given the benefit of doubt to be able to defend oneself.

The man wore a green talisman on his finger – though he swore it had simply been a green ring. Because the ring was feared, nobody wanted to touch it. So instead, the hand was cut off to be buried apart from the rest of the burnt body.

Unfortunately, the severed hand came back to life seeking its own vengeance.

Because no one foresaw the powers of the talisman, the hand now haunts the land searching for the relatives of those who took part in burning the body of the man he belonged to.

ORBS OF FIRE

In Mexican-American folklore, the presence of witches is often associated with the appearance of bright fire balls floating effortlessly in the air, bouncing from tree to tree in the middle of the night. It isn't common to catch sight of these orbs of fire and they are often mistaken as extraterrestrial UFOs.

This is why people are warned not to roam alone outside when there is a full moon out or when it is past the midnight hours. Especially if one lives out of the city limits, away from the populated suburban homes.

It is not quite clear whether these witches who travel as orbs of fire are lechuzas, or if they are from a different clan.

What is known is that when one encounters these orbs of fire balls, one is to stand still as to not distract or catch the attention of these witches.

Don't even risk trying to sneak back inside your home because if you do catch their attention and anger them, they are said to instill such an intense fear in you that you will remain frozen to the point where your limbs do not move and your eyes remain in a permanent daze.

UY, CUCUY

Ever heard of the Bogeyman?

Well, consider El Cucuy the much scarier version of it.

With red eyes and shape shifting abilities, El Cucuy has appeared to many a child in a variety of physical appearances.

El Cucuy, much like the duendes, likes to seek out badly behaved children. He'll hide under beds or in closets searching for his next meal. He camouflages into his surroundings to become invisible to the adult human eye.

You probably heard of him when you were a child yourself. Maybe you even glimpsed him, once or twice.

There are even several song rhymes of El Cucuy, some sung by mothers as a lullaby to children about how El Cucuy will come get them if they don't fall sleep.

"Go to sleep my baby,
duermete my niño.
Here comes El Cucuy,
so go to sleep my baby.

Duermete my niño,
go to sleep my baby —
because if you don't go to sleep,
El Cucuy will take you away."

MARIA MARGARITA

Maria Margarita has become a famed character in our culture, her story often shared in schools.

There are many versions to her tale, many in English and Spanish. As reiterated as these tales are, no one is sure which version is real, or if there has been more than one Mary Margaret.

She is often referred to as Bloody Mary, a nickname that well describes her ghostly attributes. This popular legend I first heard at a sleepover and have listened to one too many times.

The story states that back in the late nineteenth century, Maria Margarita survived a fire in her home. This fire had engulfed every piece of the house and had taken the lives of her dear mother and siblings. Her cruel father had intentionally set the house on fire while everyone in it slept.

His motive had been punishing his wife for her rumored infidelity. He had been told none of his children were of his own blood, but that of a secret lover. His revenge was foolishly taken, without assuring the rumor was a truth. According to his judgment, it was his right to rid himself of the woman who had made him a fool and the children who were not his.

Before the fire embellished Maria, she jumped out a bedroom window and into the obscurity of that dreadful night. Without knowing it wasn't an accident, she ran to a neighbor for help. Word got around quick about the flaming house and several families struggled to distinguish the fire.

Unfortunately, help had come too late and her family, all but her father, had perished in the fire.

Her father had supposedly been out on a business trip. He returned a few days later to find the home burnt to the ground, just as he had hoped.

With a fake pretense, he went to town and asked about his family and what had happened to his home. He threw a fit when told of the accident, but secretly fringed inside when told Maria had survived.

The town held a mass in honor of the deceased, and Maria Margarita and her father soon left town in search of a new home. They wanted to get as far possible from the memories of the dreadful fire.

The night after settling into a distant inn, her father confessed he provoked the fire for revenge, his hatred burning in his stare. Without giving her a chance to speak, he told her she was to meet the same fate as her family too.

She was tortured so vainly her spirit remains on earth as a means to revenge the deaths of her family, and her own. She has no compassion for the humanity that had so badly offended and hurt her.

Back in the 1930's, a witch was said to entrap Maria Margarita's spirit into a mirror, after the ghost had haunted and killed many people. For some reason, it is exciting for people to come face to face with this hideous ghost.

It has become a legend that if you enter a dark room and look into the mirror, repeating her name several times, the image of Maria Margarita will appear. The mirror will bleed human blood and she can tell you your future, but only after she scratches your face and tastes your blood.

THE LEAPERS OF PORT ISABEL

Maria Elena enjoyed the attention of her many admirers. She was a fair beauty and had many men rivaling for her hand in marriage. Just as soon as she'd accept a beau, she would leave him for another. It was a game she played, time and again.

But her mother warned her to be careful. Eventually, she'd loose her heart to one of them.

She thought that was the furthest from her reality. She was sure she'd never fall in love. At least, not with the men in the area. Maria Elena knew what she wanted, and that was to marry a wealthy man. Until the opportunity came along, she enjoyed the flirtatious actions a beauty like her was free to take.

The girl won over the love of any man who crossed her path, as she did with Cornelio. He had pursued her since childhood and was the first one to admit his passion for her. It took her that long to accept his proposals of dating. Maria Elena reached out to him only after she had courted every other available male who attracted her.

With Cornelio, she engaged more time. There was no other direction to turn to, for the time being at least. That is, until the right kind of man came along. The moment became a month, the month became six months, and the six months soon became a year.

That is when Cornelio asked her to marry him. Of course she refused him, with the excuse she was not ready for marriage. But we know her true intentions.

He had always been obsessed with her, but now even more so. Without realizing, she had begun to love him. Rumors spread through town that Maria Elena had finally fallen in love, but she claimed it to be just a rumor.

One day, while out for a walk, she bumped into an older man she hadn't before seen. After apologizing to the stranger, they conversed for hours. Mostly about the local attractions and their backgrounds. She was amused by his style. The elegance of his conversation made his wealth obvious.

Soon enough, she broke off the courtship with Cornelio to begin an engagement with the wealthy man. This was the type of commitment she had been waiting for and she took for granted if it didn't work out, she could return to faithful Cornelio whenever she pleased.

The days wore off and unexpectedly, she missed her young man more than she'd ever missed anybody or anything in her entire life. She wouldn't admit to herself what she felt was love. The willpower was stronger than the heart's desire. She was to marry a wealthy man, as a beauty like her deserved. Not a poor and plain boy like Cornelio.

Maria Elena avoided Cornelio. But he was not ready to give her up.

He came to her late in the eve on the night before her wedding and demanded her to return to him. She refused, despite the countless hours of his begging and crying.

It was obvious she wanted to jump into his arms. He noticed this, but she kept firm to her decision. When he finally gave up on her, he warned her if she didn't return to him by the morning, he would take his own life.

She kept firm with her decision.

The girl dressed for her wedding and the pain hit her to the gut. On the way to church, the pain hit her chest so strongly, she thought she would die. It was before entering the church she realized her love for Cornelio was indeed real, and it would have to do. Money wasn't as important to her as the love she felt.

While she turned to run to the man she loved, a cold chill settled in her heart. This is how she knew Cornelio had kept his word.

For the following weeks, she lived as a zombie, speaking no words and shedding no tears. The shock had driven her mad. Her mother prayed for her well-being every night and morning and afternoon, and in between. She just continued to pray for her daughter's sanity.

A few months had gone by and the mother was worried more than ever.

Maria Elena would speak to the air and the walls, but not to people. She wasn't her usual self, always restless. When it was discovered she'd spent the nights on Cornelio's grave, her mother cried for days. Maria Elena explained Cornelio was to return for her so they could marry on the other side.

The girl was mad.

Afraid she'd hurt herself, her family locked her in the shed where she couldn't sneak out, not even by a window.

That same night she was locked in, Cornelio walked into the room and unlocked the door with ease. When the couple passed the patio, the family was still sitting in shock of seeing the dead man alive.

Her parents followed them slowly, afraid of what they saw.

They realized they were nearing the sea, soon walking on the bridge to the island.

Her parents let out a loud shriek of fear as the younger couple looked back at them, waved, and leaped off into the black waters. Maria Elena's shawl flew in the air, but Cornelio and the girl had disappeared in midair.

For many decades, the parents told their tale, even after the bridge collapsed and a new one was built in its place. Maria Elena was filed as a missing person and because everyone knew how overprotective her parents

47

had been, they were rumored to have made up this tale.

It was believed the girl had run away to elope with some odd man. But not ever could the young couple have leaped off the bridge.

Remember, Cornelio had already been dead for months.

Oddly enough, Maria Elena was never found.

ACKNOWLEDGEMENTS

These are cuentos that belong to no one in particular – they are leyendas we have all heard in our communities and that have become a part of pop culture. Most of these cuentos I have heard from my relatives, friends, and school teachers.

I was first inspired to document these cuentos for the youth in our South Texas community at McAllen Public Library, where my peers encouraged my storytelling and provided me a platform to share these leyendas with our patrons.

The beautiful cover image, 'El Callejon Del Beso', was graciously provided for this collection by Chusy Ocala.

Some of these stories have previously been published in *Along the River III: Dark Voices from the Rio Grande*.

FOLLOW THE AUTHOR
ON SOCIAL MEDIA!

@priscilla.suarez

@suapri78501

@suapri

@suapri

https://pcsuarez.wordpress.com/

ABOUT THE AUTHOR

Priscilla Celina Suárez is the 2015-17 McAllen Poet Laureate and has been a recipient of the *Mexicasa Writing Fellowship*. A Rio Grande Valley native, her poetry is a hybrid of rancheras, polkas, pop, rock, and música internacional. A past contributor to the American Library Association's *Young Adult Library Services* magazine, she has also authored the Texas State Library's *Bilingual Programs Chapter* – allowing her an opportunity to gain experience in writing poetry, rhymes, and tongue twisters for children and teens.

Her poetry was included in *¡Juventud!: Growing up on the Border* and *Along the River III: Dark Voices from the Río Grande*. In 2003, her work was selected by the Monitor staff as 'The Best Poetry of the Year'.

BIBLIOGRAPHY
The author's work has also appeared in:

Made in the USA
Lexington, KY
25 October 2019